50 Best Pasta and Cheese Recipes

By: Kelly Johnson

Table of Contents

- Mac and Cheese
- Four-Cheese Pasta Bake
- Baked Ziti with Ricotta
- Spinach and Ricotta Stuffed Shells
- Cheese Ravioli in Creamy Tomato Sauce
- Fettuccine Alfredo
- Pesto Mac and Cheese
- Baked Penne with Mozzarella
- Cheese Tortellini with Garlic Butter
- Pasta Carbonara
- Baked Gnocchi with Parmesan
- Cheese Lasagna
- Pasta with Ricotta and Lemon
- Creamy Goat Cheese Pasta
- Baked Manicotti
- Pasta Primavera with Parmesan
- Parmesan-Crusted Pasta

- Shrimp and Feta Pasta
- Three-Cheese Stuffed Shells
- Feta and Spinach Pasta
- Creamy Cheddar Pasta
- Baked Rigatoni with Bechamel
- Gnocchi with Gorgonzola Cream Sauce
- Cheese and Bacon Stuffed Pasta
- Baked Macaroni and Cheese
- Cheesy Stuffed Bell Peppers
- Cheesy Pasta Casserole
- Ricotta and Spinach Lasagna
- Bacon-Cheddar Pasta
- Parmesan and Herb Pasta
- Cheese Fondue Pasta
- Pasta with Blue Cheese Sauce
- Cheddar and Broccoli Pasta Bake
- Pappardelle with Ricotta
- Spaghetti with Creamy Cheese Sauce
- Mozzarella-Stuffed Meatballs with Pasta

- Pasta with Gorgonzola and Walnuts
- Ravioli with Parmesan Cream Sauce
- Pasta with Brie and Mushrooms
- Mac and Cheese with Bacon
- Pasta with Ricotta and Spinach Sauce
- Pesto and Parmesan Pasta
- Pasta with Roasted Garlic and Parmesan
- Cheddar and Chive Pasta
- Creamy Feta Pasta
- Truffle Mac and Cheese
- Pasta with Burrata and Cherry Tomatoes
- Pasta with Pecorino and Arugula
- Cheesy Garlic Bread Pasta
- Ziti with Mozzarella and Marinara

Mac and Cheese

Ingredients:

- 8 oz pasta (elbow or other preferred shape)
- 2 tbsp butter
- 2 tbsp flour
- 2 cups milk
- 2 cups shredded cheddar cheese
- 1/2 cup grated parmesan cheese
- Salt and pepper
- 1/2 tsp mustard powder (optional)

Instructions:

1. Cook pasta and set aside.
2. In a saucepan, melt butter and whisk in flour to form a roux.
3. Slowly add milk while whisking to avoid lumps.
4. Stir in cheddar and parmesan cheese, and cook until the sauce thickens.
5. Combine with the cooked pasta and season with salt, pepper, and mustard powder for a deeper flavor.
6. Serve hot and enjoy!

Four-Cheese Pasta Bake

Ingredients:

- 8 oz pasta (penne or rigatoni)
- 2 tbsp butter
- 2 tbsp flour
- 2 cups milk
- 1 cup shredded mozzarella cheese
- 1 cup shredded cheddar cheese
- 1/2 cup grated parmesan cheese
- 1/2 cup ricotta cheese
- Salt and pepper
- 1/2 cup breadcrumbs

Instructions:

1. Cook pasta and set aside.
2. In a saucepan, melt butter and whisk in flour.
3. Gradually add milk and cook until thickened.
4. Stir in all cheeses (mozzarella, cheddar, parmesan, and ricotta) and season with salt and pepper.
5. Mix cheese sauce with pasta and transfer to a baking dish.

6. Top with breadcrumbs and bake at 375°F for 20–25 minutes until golden and bubbly.

Baked Ziti with Ricotta

Ingredients:

- 8 oz ziti pasta
- 2 cups marinara sauce
- 1/2 cup ricotta cheese
- 2 cups shredded mozzarella cheese
- 1/4 cup grated parmesan cheese
- 1 tbsp chopped basil (optional)
- Salt and pepper

Instructions:

1. Cook ziti and drain.
2. In a large bowl, mix pasta, marinara sauce, ricotta, mozzarella, and parmesan.
3. Season with salt, pepper, and basil.
4. Transfer to a baking dish and top with extra mozzarella and parmesan.
5. Bake at 375°F for 20 minutes until cheese is bubbly and golden.

Spinach and Ricotta Stuffed Shells

Ingredients:

- 12 jumbo pasta shells
- 1 cup ricotta cheese
- 1/2 cup shredded mozzarella cheese
- 1 cup cooked spinach, squeezed dry
- 1/4 cup grated parmesan cheese
- 2 cups marinara sauce
- Salt and pepper

Instructions:

1. Cook pasta shells and set aside to cool.
2. In a bowl, mix ricotta, mozzarella, spinach, parmesan, salt, and pepper.
3. Stuff the shells with the cheese-spinach mixture.
4. Pour marinara sauce into a baking dish and place the stuffed shells on top.
5. Cover with foil and bake at 375°F for 25 minutes, removing foil for the last 5 minutes to brown the cheese.

Cheese Ravioli in Creamy Tomato Sauce

Ingredients:

- 1 package cheese ravioli
- 2 tbsp butter
- 2 cloves garlic, minced
- 1 can (14.5 oz) crushed tomatoes
- 1/2 cup heavy cream
- 1/2 tsp Italian seasoning
- 1/4 cup grated parmesan cheese
- Salt and pepper

Instructions:

1. Cook ravioli according to package instructions.
2. In a pan, melt butter and sauté garlic until fragrant.
3. Add crushed tomatoes, heavy cream, and Italian seasoning.
4. Simmer for 5–7 minutes until thickened.
5. Stir in parmesan and season with salt and pepper.
6. Toss cooked ravioli with the creamy tomato sauce and serve.

Fettuccine Alfredo

Ingredients:

- 8 oz fettuccine pasta
- 2 tbsp butter
- 1 cup heavy cream
- 1 1/2 cups shredded parmesan cheese
- 1/2 tsp garlic powder
- Salt and pepper

Instructions:

1. Cook fettuccine and set aside.
2. In a pan, melt butter and add heavy cream.
3. Stir in parmesan cheese and garlic powder.
4. Cook on low until the sauce thickens.
5. Toss cooked pasta in the Alfredo sauce and season with salt and pepper.
6. Serve hot, topped with extra parmesan and parsley.

Pesto Mac and Cheese

Ingredients:

- 8 oz pasta
- 1/4 cup pesto sauce
- 2 tbsp butter
- 2 tbsp flour
- 2 cups milk
- 2 cups shredded mozzarella cheese
- Salt and pepper

Instructions:

1. Cook pasta and set aside.
2. In a saucepan, melt butter and whisk in flour.
3. Slowly add milk, stirring to avoid lumps.
4. Stir in mozzarella cheese and pesto sauce.
5. Combine with pasta and season with salt and pepper.
6. Serve hot, garnished with extra pesto.

Baked Penne with Mozzarella

Ingredients:

- 8 oz penne pasta
- 2 cups marinara sauce
- 2 cups shredded mozzarella cheese
- 1/2 cup grated parmesan cheese
- 1/4 cup chopped basil (optional)
- Salt and pepper

Instructions:

1. Cook penne and set aside.
2. Mix pasta with marinara sauce and mozzarella cheese.
3. Transfer to a baking dish and top with parmesan cheese.
4. Bake at 375°F for 20–25 minutes until cheese is melted and bubbly.
5. Garnish with basil before serving.

Cheese Tortellini with Garlic Butter

Ingredients:

- 8 oz cheese tortellini
- 4 tbsp butter
- 2 cloves garlic, minced
- 1/4 cup grated parmesan cheese
- Salt and pepper
- Fresh parsley (optional)

Instructions:

1. Cook tortellini according to package instructions and set aside.
2. In a pan, melt butter and sauté garlic until fragrant.
3. Toss cooked tortellini in the garlic butter and season with salt and pepper.
4. Sprinkle with parmesan and fresh parsley before serving.

Pasta Carbonara

Ingredients:

- 8 oz pasta (spaghetti or fettuccine)
- 4 oz pancetta or bacon, diced
- 2 large eggs
- 1 cup grated parmesan cheese
- 1/2 cup heavy cream
- 1 tsp garlic powder
- Salt and pepper
- Fresh parsley (optional)

Instructions:

1. Cook pasta according to package instructions.
2. While the pasta is cooking, sauté pancetta or bacon in a pan until crispy.
3. In a bowl, whisk together eggs, parmesan cheese, heavy cream, garlic powder, salt, and pepper.
4. Drain pasta, reserving some pasta water.
5. Toss pasta in the pan with pancetta.
6. Gradually stir in the egg mixture, adding a bit of reserved pasta water to create a creamy sauce.
7. Serve immediately, garnished with fresh parsley.

Baked Gnocchi with Parmesan

Ingredients:

- 16 oz gnocchi (store-bought or homemade)
- 2 cups marinara sauce
- 1 cup shredded mozzarella cheese
- 1/2 cup grated parmesan cheese
- 1/4 tsp garlic powder
- Fresh basil (optional)

Instructions:

1. Preheat oven to 375°F (190°C).
2. Cook gnocchi according to package instructions and drain.
3. In a baking dish, spread marinara sauce on the bottom, then layer with cooked gnocchi.
4. Sprinkle mozzarella and parmesan cheese on top, followed by garlic powder.
5. Bake for 20-25 minutes until bubbly and golden.
6. Garnish with fresh basil and serve.

Cheese Lasagna

Ingredients:

- 9 lasagna noodles, cooked and drained
- 2 cups ricotta cheese
- 2 cups shredded mozzarella cheese
- 1/2 cup grated parmesan cheese
- 1 jar marinara sauce
- 1 egg
- 2 tbsp chopped basil
- Salt and pepper

Instructions:

1. Preheat oven to 375°F (190°C).
2. Mix ricotta cheese, egg, basil, salt, and pepper in a bowl.
3. Spread a thin layer of marinara sauce in a baking dish.
4. Layer lasagna noodles, ricotta mixture, mozzarella, parmesan, and marinara sauce. Repeat layers.
5. Finish with a layer of mozzarella and parmesan on top.
6. Cover with foil and bake for 30 minutes.
7. Uncover and bake for an additional 10-15 minutes until golden and bubbly.

Pasta with Ricotta and Lemon

Ingredients:

- 8 oz pasta (spaghetti or fettuccine)
- 1 cup ricotta cheese
- Zest and juice of 1 lemon
- 2 tbsp olive oil
- 1/2 cup grated parmesan cheese
- Salt and pepper
- Fresh basil or parsley (optional)

Instructions:

1. Cook pasta according to package instructions.
2. In a bowl, mix ricotta, lemon zest, lemon juice, olive oil, parmesan, salt, and pepper.
3. Drain pasta, reserving some pasta water.
4. Toss pasta in ricotta mixture, adding a bit of reserved pasta water to create a creamy sauce.
5. Serve with fresh basil or parsley and extra parmesan.

Creamy Goat Cheese Pasta

Ingredients:

- 8 oz pasta (penne or spaghetti)
- 4 oz goat cheese, crumbled
- 1 cup heavy cream
- 1/2 cup chicken broth
- 2 tbsp olive oil
- 2 cloves garlic, minced
- Salt and pepper
- Fresh thyme (optional)

Instructions:

1. Cook pasta according to package instructions.
2. In a pan, heat olive oil and sauté garlic until fragrant.
3. Add chicken broth and heavy cream, simmering for 5 minutes.
4. Stir in goat cheese and let it melt into the sauce.
5. Season with salt and pepper.
6. Toss cooked pasta in the creamy goat cheese sauce.
7. Garnish with fresh thyme and serve.

Baked Manicotti

Ingredients:

- 12 manicotti shells
- 2 cups ricotta cheese
- 1 cup shredded mozzarella cheese
- 1/4 cup grated parmesan cheese
- 1 egg
- 2 cups marinara sauce
- Salt and pepper
- Fresh basil (optional)

Instructions:

1. Preheat oven to 375°F (190°C).
2. Cook manicotti shells according to package instructions.
3. In a bowl, mix ricotta, mozzarella, parmesan, egg, salt, and pepper.
4. Stuff each manicotti shell with the cheese mixture.
5. Spread marinara sauce in a baking dish, then place stuffed shells on top.
6. Cover with foil and bake for 25 minutes.
7. Uncover, sprinkle with extra cheese, and bake for another 10 minutes until golden.

Pasta Primavera with Parmesan

Ingredients:

- 8 oz pasta (penne or fusilli)
- 1 cup mixed vegetables (e.g., bell peppers, zucchini, cherry tomatoes)
- 2 tbsp olive oil
- 1/2 cup grated parmesan cheese
- 1 tbsp chopped basil
- Salt and pepper

Instructions:

1. Cook pasta according to package instructions.
2. In a pan, heat olive oil and sauté mixed vegetables until tender.
3. Toss cooked pasta with the sautéed vegetables and parmesan cheese.
4. Season with salt, pepper, and basil.
5. Serve with extra parmesan.

Parmesan-Crusted Pasta

Ingredients:

- 8 oz pasta (spaghetti or penne)
- 2 tbsp butter
- 1 cup grated parmesan cheese
- 1/4 cup breadcrumbs
- 2 tbsp olive oil
- Salt and pepper

Instructions:

1. Cook pasta and set aside.
2. In a pan, melt butter and sauté breadcrumbs until golden and crispy.
3. Stir in parmesan cheese and toss with the cooked pasta.
4. Drizzle with olive oil, season with salt and pepper, and serve.

Shrimp and Feta Pasta

Ingredients:

- 8 oz pasta (linguine or spaghetti)
- 1 lb shrimp, peeled and deveined
- 1 tbsp olive oil
- 2 cloves garlic, minced
- 1 cup crumbled feta cheese
- 1/2 cup cherry tomatoes, halved
- 1 tbsp chopped parsley
- Salt and pepper

Instructions:

1. Cook pasta according to package instructions.
2. In a pan, heat olive oil and sauté garlic until fragrant.
3. Add shrimp and cook until pink.
4. Toss cooked pasta with shrimp, feta cheese, cherry tomatoes, and parsley.
5. Season with salt and pepper and serve.

Three-Cheese Stuffed Shells

Ingredients:

- 12 jumbo pasta shells
- 1 cup ricotta cheese
- 1 cup shredded mozzarella cheese
- 1/2 cup grated parmesan cheese
- 1 egg
- 2 cups marinara sauce
- 1 tbsp chopped basil
- Salt and pepper

Instructions:

1. Preheat oven to 375°F (190°C).
2. Cook pasta shells according to package instructions and set aside.
3. In a bowl, mix ricotta, mozzarella, parmesan, egg, basil, salt, and pepper.
4. Stuff each shell with the cheese mixture.
5. Spread marinara sauce on the bottom of a baking dish, then place the stuffed shells on top.
6. Cover with foil and bake for 25 minutes.
7. Uncover, top with extra cheese, and bake for another 10 minutes until golden.

Feta and Spinach Pasta

Ingredients:

- 8 oz pasta (penne or fusilli)
- 2 cups fresh spinach, chopped
- 1/2 cup crumbled feta cheese
- 2 tbsp olive oil
- 2 cloves garlic, minced
- 1/2 cup chicken broth
- Salt and pepper

Instructions:

1. Cook pasta according to package instructions and set aside.
2. In a pan, heat olive oil and sauté garlic until fragrant.
3. Add spinach and cook until wilted.
4. Stir in chicken broth, crumbled feta, and season with salt and pepper.
5. Toss cooked pasta in the spinach and feta sauce.
6. Serve with extra feta on top.

Creamy Cheddar Pasta

Ingredients:

- 8 oz pasta (macaroni or shells)
- 1 cup shredded cheddar cheese
- 1/2 cup heavy cream
- 1/4 cup milk
- 2 tbsp butter
- Salt and pepper
- 1/2 tsp garlic powder (optional)

Instructions:

1. Cook pasta according to package instructions.
2. In a pan, melt butter over medium heat.
3. Add heavy cream and milk, stirring to combine.
4. Slowly stir in cheddar cheese until melted and smooth.
5. Season with salt, pepper, and garlic powder.
6. Toss cooked pasta in the creamy cheddar sauce and serve.

Baked Rigatoni with Bechamel

Ingredients:

- 1 lb rigatoni pasta
- 2 cups bechamel sauce (see below)
- 1 1/2 cups marinara sauce
- 1 1/2 cups shredded mozzarella cheese
- 1/2 cup grated parmesan cheese
- Salt and pepper

Bechamel Sauce:

- 2 tbsp butter
- 2 tbsp flour
- 2 cups milk
- Salt and pepper

Instructions:

1. Preheat oven to 375°F (190°C).
2. Cook rigatoni pasta according to package instructions.
3. To make bechamel, melt butter in a saucepan, then whisk in flour and cook for 1 minute.
4. Gradually add milk, whisking constantly, until thickened. Season with salt and pepper.

5. Mix rigatoni with bechamel sauce and marinara sauce.

6. Pour into a baking dish, top with mozzarella and parmesan, and bake for 20 minutes until bubbly.

Gnocchi with Gorgonzola Cream Sauce

Ingredients:

- 1 lb gnocchi
- 1/2 cup heavy cream
- 1/2 cup crumbled gorgonzola cheese
- 1 tbsp olive oil
- 2 cloves garlic, minced
- Salt and pepper
- Fresh parsley (optional)

Instructions:

1. Cook gnocchi according to package instructions and set aside.
2. In a pan, heat olive oil and sauté garlic until fragrant.
3. Stir in heavy cream and bring to a simmer.
4. Add crumbled gorgonzola cheese and stir until melted and smooth.
5. Season with salt and pepper.
6. Toss cooked gnocchi in the creamy gorgonzola sauce and serve with fresh parsley.

Cheese and Bacon Stuffed Pasta

Ingredients:

- 12 jumbo pasta shells
- 6 slices bacon, cooked and crumbled
- 1 cup ricotta cheese
- 1/2 cup shredded mozzarella cheese
- 1/4 cup grated parmesan cheese
- 1/4 tsp garlic powder
- Salt and pepper
- 2 cups marinara sauce

Instructions:

1. Preheat oven to 375°F (190°C).
2. Cook pasta shells according to package instructions.
3. In a bowl, mix ricotta, mozzarella, parmesan, bacon, garlic powder, salt, and pepper.
4. Stuff each shell with the cheese and bacon mixture.
5. Spread marinara sauce in the bottom of a baking dish and arrange stuffed shells on top.
6. Bake for 20-25 minutes until bubbly and golden.

Baked Macaroni and Cheese

Ingredients:

- 8 oz elbow macaroni
- 2 cups shredded cheddar cheese
- 1/2 cup grated parmesan cheese
- 1 cup milk
- 2 tbsp butter
- 2 tbsp flour
- 1/2 tsp mustard powder
- Salt and pepper
- 1/2 cup breadcrumbs

Instructions:

1. Preheat oven to 375°F (190°C).
2. Cook macaroni according to package instructions and set aside.
3. In a saucepan, melt butter and whisk in flour to create a roux.
4. Gradually add milk, whisking constantly until thickened.
5. Stir in cheddar cheese, parmesan, mustard powder, salt, and pepper.
6. Mix the cooked macaroni with the cheese sauce and pour into a baking dish.
7. Top with breadcrumbs and bake for 20 minutes until golden.

Cheesy Stuffed Bell Peppers

Ingredients:

- 4 bell peppers, tops cut off and seeds removed
- 1 cup cooked rice
- 1 cup shredded cheddar cheese
- 1/2 cup ricotta cheese
- 1/4 cup grated parmesan cheese
- 1 cup marinara sauce
- Salt and pepper

Instructions:

1. Preheat oven to 375°F (190°C).
2. Blanch bell peppers in boiling water for 2-3 minutes, then drain.
3. In a bowl, mix rice, cheddar, ricotta, parmesan, salt, and pepper.
4. Stuff the peppers with the cheese and rice mixture.
5. Place peppers in a baking dish and top with marinara sauce.
6. Cover with foil and bake for 25-30 minutes.
7. Uncover and bake for an additional 10 minutes until bubbly.

Cheesy Pasta Casserole

Ingredients:

- 8 oz pasta (your choice)
- 2 cups shredded cheddar cheese
- 1 cup ricotta cheese
- 1/2 cup grated parmesan cheese
- 1/2 cup sour cream
- 2 cups marinara sauce
- Salt and pepper
- 1/2 cup breadcrumbs

Instructions:

1. Preheat oven to 375°F (190°C).
2. Cook pasta according to package instructions and set aside.
3. In a bowl, combine ricotta, cheddar, parmesan, sour cream, salt, and pepper.
4. Mix the cooked pasta with the cheese mixture and marinara sauce.
5. Pour the mixture into a baking dish and top with breadcrumbs.
6. Bake for 25-30 minutes until bubbly and golden.

Ricotta and Spinach Lasagna

Ingredients:

- 9 lasagna noodles
- 2 cups ricotta cheese
- 2 cups spinach, chopped
- 1 1/2 cups marinara sauce
- 2 cups shredded mozzarella cheese
- 1/4 cup grated parmesan cheese
- 1 egg
- Salt and pepper

Instructions:

1. Preheat oven to 375°F (190°C).
2. Cook lasagna noodles according to package instructions.
3. In a bowl, combine ricotta, spinach, egg, salt, and pepper.
4. In a baking dish, spread a thin layer of marinara sauce, then layer lasagna noodles, ricotta mixture, mozzarella, and parmesan. Repeat layers until ingredients are used up.
5. Finish with mozzarella on top and bake for 30-40 minutes.

Bacon-Cheddar Pasta

Ingredients:

- 8 oz pasta (penne or shells)
- 6 slices bacon, cooked and crumbled
- 1 cup shredded cheddar cheese
- 1/2 cup heavy cream
- 2 tbsp butter
- Salt and pepper

Instructions:

1. Cook pasta according to package instructions.
2. In a pan, melt butter and stir in heavy cream.
3. Add cheddar cheese and stir until melted.
4. Mix in cooked pasta and bacon.
5. Season with salt and pepper, then serve.

Parmesan and Herb Pasta

Ingredients:

- 8 oz pasta (spaghetti or fettuccine)
- 1 cup grated parmesan cheese
- 2 tbsp butter
- 1/4 cup olive oil
- 1 tsp garlic powder
- 1 tbsp fresh herbs (basil, oregano, or thyme)
- Salt and pepper

Instructions:

1. Cook pasta according to package instructions.
2. In a pan, heat olive oil and butter.
3. Add garlic powder and fresh herbs, stirring for 1-2 minutes.
4. Toss the cooked pasta in the sauce, adding parmesan, salt, and pepper.
5. Serve with extra parmesan and herbs on top.

Cheese Fondue Pasta

Ingredients:

- 8 oz pasta (penne or rotini)
- 1 cup Swiss cheese, shredded
- 1/2 cup Gruyère cheese, shredded
- 1/2 cup white wine (optional)
- 1/2 cup heavy cream
- 1 tbsp butter
- Salt and pepper

Instructions:

1. Cook pasta according to package instructions.
2. In a pan, melt butter and stir in heavy cream and wine (if using).
3. Add the shredded cheeses and stir until smooth and melted.
4. Toss the cooked pasta in the cheese sauce.
5. Season with salt and pepper, then serve.

Pasta with Blue Cheese Sauce

Ingredients:

- 8 oz pasta (spaghetti or penne)
- 1/2 cup crumbled blue cheese
- 1/2 cup heavy cream
- 1 tbsp butter
- 1 tbsp olive oil
- Salt and pepper

Instructions:

1. Cook pasta according to package instructions.
2. In a pan, melt butter and olive oil.
3. Add heavy cream and crumbled blue cheese, stirring until smooth.
4. Toss the cooked pasta in the blue cheese sauce.
5. Season with salt and pepper, then serve.

Cheddar and Broccoli Pasta Bake

Ingredients:

- 8 oz pasta (elbow macaroni or penne)
- 1 1/2 cups shredded cheddar cheese
- 1 cup broccoli florets, steamed
- 1/2 cup milk
- 2 tbsp butter
- 2 tbsp flour
- Salt and pepper
- 1/2 cup breadcrumbs

Instructions:

1. Preheat oven to 375°F (190°C).
2. Cook pasta according to package instructions and steam broccoli.
3. In a pan, melt butter, then whisk in flour to create a roux.
4. Gradually add milk, stirring until thickened.
5. Stir in cheddar cheese, salt, and pepper.
6. Mix pasta, broccoli, and cheese sauce, then pour into a baking dish.
7. Top with breadcrumbs and bake for 20-25 minutes.

Pappardelle with Ricotta

Ingredients:

- 8 oz pappardelle pasta
- 1 cup ricotta cheese
- 2 tbsp olive oil
- 1/2 cup grated parmesan cheese
- Salt and pepper
- Fresh basil for garnish

Instructions:

1. Cook pappardelle according to package instructions.
2. In a pan, heat olive oil and stir in ricotta cheese.
3. Toss cooked pasta in the ricotta mixture, adding parmesan, salt, and pepper.
4. Garnish with fresh basil and serve.

Spaghetti with Creamy Cheese Sauce

Ingredients:

- 8 oz spaghetti
- 1 cup heavy cream
- 1/2 cup shredded parmesan cheese
- 2 tbsp butter
- 2 cloves garlic, minced
- Salt and pepper

Instructions:

1. Cook spaghetti according to package instructions.
2. In a pan, melt butter and sauté garlic until fragrant.
3. Add heavy cream and bring to a simmer.
4. Stir in parmesan cheese until melted and smooth.
5. Toss the cooked spaghetti in the creamy cheese sauce.
6. Season with salt and pepper, then serve.

Mozzarella-Stuffed Meatballs with Pasta

Ingredients:

- 1 lb ground beef
- 1/2 cup breadcrumbs
- 1/4 cup grated parmesan cheese
- 1 egg
- 1 tsp garlic powder
- Salt and pepper
- 1 cup fresh mozzarella, cut into cubes
- 2 cups marinara sauce
- 8 oz spaghetti or your favorite pasta
- Fresh basil (optional)

Instructions:

1. Preheat oven to 375°F (190°C).
2. In a bowl, mix ground beef, breadcrumbs, parmesan, egg, garlic powder, salt, and pepper.
3. Take a small amount of the beef mixture, flatten it, and place a cube of mozzarella in the center. Roll into a meatball.
4. Place the meatballs on a baking sheet and bake for 20 minutes.
5. In a pan, heat marinara sauce and add the meatballs. Simmer for 10 minutes.

6. Cook pasta according to package instructions.

7. Serve meatballs over pasta and garnish with fresh basil if desired.

Pasta with Gorgonzola and Walnuts

Ingredients:

- 8 oz pasta (penne or fettuccine)
- 1/2 cup crumbled Gorgonzola cheese
- 1/2 cup heavy cream
- 1 tbsp olive oil
- 1/4 cup walnuts, chopped
- 1/4 cup grated parmesan cheese
- Salt and pepper
- Fresh parsley for garnish

Instructions:

1. Cook pasta according to package instructions.
2. In a pan, heat olive oil and sauté walnuts until lightly toasted.
3. Add heavy cream to the pan and bring to a simmer. Stir in Gorgonzola cheese until melted and smooth.
4. Toss the cooked pasta in the sauce, adding parmesan, salt, and pepper.
5. Garnish with fresh parsley and serve.

Ravioli with Parmesan Cream Sauce

Ingredients:

- 1 package of cheese ravioli
- 1 cup heavy cream
- 1/2 cup grated parmesan cheese
- 2 tbsp butter
- 2 cloves garlic, minced
- Salt and pepper
- Fresh basil for garnish

Instructions:

1. Cook ravioli according to package instructions.
2. In a pan, melt butter and sauté garlic until fragrant.
3. Add heavy cream and bring to a simmer.
4. Stir in parmesan cheese until the sauce is creamy and smooth.
5. Toss the cooked ravioli in the cream sauce.
6. Season with salt and pepper, and garnish with fresh basil before serving.

Pasta with Brie and Mushrooms

Ingredients:

- 8 oz pasta (fettuccine or penne)
- 1 cup Brie cheese, rind removed and cubed
- 1 cup mushrooms, sliced
- 1/2 cup heavy cream
- 2 tbsp olive oil
- 1 tbsp fresh thyme
- Salt and pepper

Instructions:

1. Cook pasta according to package instructions.
2. In a pan, heat olive oil and sauté mushrooms until soft.
3. Add heavy cream and bring to a simmer.
4. Stir in Brie cheese until melted and smooth.
5. Toss the cooked pasta in the sauce, adding fresh thyme, salt, and pepper.
6. Serve with extra thyme on top.

Mac and Cheese with Bacon

Ingredients:

- 8 oz elbow macaroni
- 2 cups shredded cheddar cheese
- 1/2 cup milk
- 1 tbsp butter
- 6 slices bacon, cooked and crumbled
- Salt and pepper
- 1/4 cup breadcrumbs (optional)

Instructions:

1. Cook macaroni according to package instructions.
2. In a pan, melt butter and add milk, stirring until heated.
3. Add shredded cheddar cheese and stir until melted.
4. Mix in cooked macaroni and crumbled bacon.
5. Season with salt and pepper, and top with breadcrumbs if desired.
6. Serve immediately.

Pasta with Ricotta and Spinach Sauce

Ingredients:

- 8 oz pasta (penne or rigatoni)
- 1 cup ricotta cheese
- 2 cups spinach, cooked and chopped
- 1/4 cup grated parmesan cheese
- 1/2 cup heavy cream
- 2 cloves garlic, minced
- Salt and pepper

Instructions:

1. Cook pasta according to package instructions.
2. In a pan, sauté garlic until fragrant. Add spinach and cook for 2 minutes.
3. Stir in ricotta cheese and heavy cream, cooking until heated through.
4. Toss the cooked pasta in the ricotta-spinach sauce, adding parmesan, salt, and pepper.
5. Serve with extra parmesan on top.

Pesto and Parmesan Pasta

Ingredients:

- 8 oz pasta (spaghetti or penne)
- 1/2 cup pesto sauce
- 1/4 cup grated parmesan cheese
- Salt and pepper

Instructions:

1. Cook pasta according to package instructions.
2. Toss the cooked pasta with pesto sauce, adding parmesan, salt, and pepper.
3. Serve with additional parmesan and fresh basil if desired.

Pasta with Roasted Garlic and Parmesan

Ingredients:

- 8 oz pasta (linguine or spaghetti)
- 1 bulb garlic
- 1/4 cup olive oil
- 1/2 cup grated parmesan cheese
- Salt and pepper
- Fresh parsley for garnish

Instructions:

1. Preheat oven to 400°F (200°C). Cut the top off the garlic bulb, drizzle with olive oil, and wrap in foil. Roast for 25-30 minutes until soft.
2. Cook pasta according to package instructions.
3. Squeeze the roasted garlic out of the skins and mash.
4. Toss the cooked pasta with mashed garlic, parmesan, salt, and pepper.
5. Garnish with fresh parsley and serve.

Cheddar and Chive Pasta

Ingredients:

- 8 oz pasta (penne or rotini)
- 1 cup shredded cheddar cheese
- 1/2 cup heavy cream
- 2 tbsp butter
- 1/4 cup chopped fresh chives
- Salt and pepper

Instructions:

1. Cook pasta according to package instructions.
2. In a pan, melt butter and add heavy cream, stirring until heated.
3. Stir in cheddar cheese until melted and smooth.
4. Toss the cooked pasta in the creamy cheese sauce, adding chives, salt, and pepper.
5. Serve with extra chives on top.

Creamy Feta Pasta

Ingredients:

- 8 oz pasta (penne or fusilli)
- 1/2 cup feta cheese
- 1/4 cup heavy cream
- 2 tbsp olive oil
- 1 clove garlic, minced
- 1/4 cup fresh basil, chopped
- Salt and pepper
- Fresh lemon juice (optional)

Instructions:

1. Cook pasta according to package instructions.
2. In a pan, heat olive oil and sauté garlic until fragrant.
3. Add heavy cream and bring to a simmer. Stir in feta cheese until creamy.
4. Toss the cooked pasta in the creamy feta sauce, adding basil, salt, and pepper.
5. Optionally, squeeze fresh lemon juice over the top and serve.

Truffle Mac and Cheese

Ingredients:

- 8 oz elbow macaroni
- 1 cup shredded sharp cheddar cheese
- 1 cup shredded Gruyère cheese
- 1/2 cup heavy cream
- 2 tbsp truffle oil
- 2 tbsp butter
- 1 tbsp all-purpose flour
- Salt and pepper
- Fresh parsley for garnish

Instructions:

1. Cook macaroni according to package instructions.
2. In a saucepan, melt butter and add flour to create a roux. Stir for 1-2 minutes.
3. Gradually add heavy cream, whisking until the sauce thickens.
4. Stir in cheddar and Gruyère cheese until melted.
5. Mix in truffle oil, salt, and pepper to taste.
6. Toss the cooked macaroni in the truffle cheese sauce and garnish with fresh parsley.

Pasta with Burrata and Cherry Tomatoes

Ingredients:

- 8 oz pasta (spaghetti or linguine)
- 1 ball of burrata cheese
- 1 cup cherry tomatoes, halved
- 2 tbsp olive oil
- 2 cloves garlic, minced
- Fresh basil leaves
- Salt and pepper
- Balsamic glaze (optional)

Instructions:

1. Cook pasta according to package instructions.
2. In a pan, heat olive oil and sauté garlic until fragrant. Add cherry tomatoes and cook until they soften.
3. Toss the cooked pasta in the pan with tomatoes and garlic. Season with salt and pepper.
4. Tear the burrata into pieces and add it to the pasta.
5. Garnish with fresh basil and drizzle with balsamic glaze if desired.

Pasta with Pecorino and Arugula

Ingredients:

- 8 oz pasta (spaghetti or penne)
- 1/2 cup Pecorino Romano cheese, grated
- 2 cups fresh arugula
- 1/4 cup olive oil
- 1 clove garlic, minced
- 1/4 cup pine nuts, toasted
- Salt and pepper

Instructions:

1. Cook pasta according to package instructions.
2. In a pan, heat olive oil and sauté garlic until fragrant.
3. Toss the cooked pasta in the pan with garlic and olive oil.
4. Add grated Pecorino cheese, arugula, and pine nuts. Toss until the arugula wilts.
5. Season with salt and pepper and serve immediately.

Cheesy Garlic Bread Pasta

Ingredients:

- 8 oz pasta (penne or rotini)
- 1/2 cup grated mozzarella cheese
- 1/4 cup grated parmesan cheese
- 2 tbsp butter
- 1 clove garlic, minced
- 1/2 cup breadcrumbs
- 1/4 tsp garlic powder
- Fresh parsley for garnish

Instructions:

1. Cook pasta according to package instructions.
2. In a pan, melt butter and sauté garlic until fragrant.
3. Stir in breadcrumbs and garlic powder, cooking until crispy.
4. Toss the cooked pasta in the pan with garlic butter.
5. Sprinkle mozzarella and parmesan cheese on top. Toss to melt.
6. Garnish with fresh parsley and serve.

Ziti with Mozzarella and Marinara

Ingredients:

- 8 oz ziti pasta
- 2 cups marinara sauce
- 1 cup shredded mozzarella cheese
- 1/4 cup grated parmesan cheese
- Fresh basil for garnish
- Salt and pepper

Instructions:

1. Cook ziti according to package instructions.
2. In a pan, heat marinara sauce until simmering.
3. Toss the cooked ziti in the marinara sauce.
4. Add mozzarella cheese and stir until melted.
5. Top with grated parmesan and fresh basil.
6. Serve immediately.

www.ingramcontent.com/pod-product-compliance
Lightning Source LLC
LaVergne TN
LVHW081321060526
838201LV00055B/2396